NTSB/RAR-07/03
PB2007-916303
Notation 7937A
Adopted October 16, 2007

I0428126

Railroad Accident Report

Derailment of Washington Metropolitan Area Transit
Authority Train near the Mt. Vernon Square Station
Washington, D.C.
January 7, 2007

**National
Transportation
Safety Board**

490 L'Enfant Plaza, S.W.
Washington, D.C. 20594

National Transportation Safety Board. 2007. Derailment of Washington Metropolitan Area Transit Authority Train near the Mt. Vernon Square Station, Washington, D.C., January 7, 2007. Railroad Accident Report NTSB/RAR-07/03. Washington, DC.

Abstract: On January 7, 2007, about 3:45 p.m. eastern standard time, northbound Washington Metropolitan Area Transit Authority Metrorail train 504 derailed one car as the train traversed a crossover from track 2 to track 1. The accident occurred in an underground tunnel on the Metrorail Green Line near the Mt. Vernon Square 7th Street-Convention Center station at chain marker E2 23+28. The train was traveling about 18 mph as it approached the station. The train consisted of six cars. The fifth car from the head end of the train derailed. About 80 passengers were on board at the time of the accident. Twenty-three passengers were transported to local hospitals for treatment and released. Emergency response personnel from Washington, D.C., provided the on-scene treatment and transportation of the injured passengers.

The safety issues identified in this accident are wheel-truing procedures, mitigating measures for wheel climb derailments, and Washington Metropolitan Area Transit Authority interdepartmental coordination.

As a result of its investigation of this accident, the National Transportation Safety Board makes recommendations to the Washington Metropolitan Area Transit Authority.

Contents

ACRONYMS AND ABBREVIATIONS

APTA	American Public Transportation Association
BART	Bay Area Rapid Transit District
CAF	Construcciones Y Auxiliar de Ferrocarriles
L/V	lateral-to-vertical
Mt. Vernon Square	Mt. Vernon Square 7th Street-Convention Center
OCC	Operations Central Control
psi	pounds per square inch
sec	second
TCRP	Transit Cooperative Research Program
TTCI	Transportation Technology Center Incorporated
WMATA	Washington Metropolitan Area Transit Authority
WRLD	wheel/rail load detector

EXECUTIVE SUMMARY

On January 7, 2007, about 3:45 p.m. eastern standard time, northbound Washington Metropolitan Area Transit Authority Metrorail train 504 derailed one car as the train traversed a crossover from track 2 to track 1. The accident occurred in an underground tunnel on the Metrorail Green Line near the Mt. Vernon Square 7th Street-Convention Center (Mt. Vernon Square) station at chain marker E2 23+28. The train was traveling about 18 mph as it approached the station.

The train consisted of six cars. The fifth car from the head end of the train derailed. About 80 passengers were on board at the time of the accident. Twenty-three passengers were transported to local hospitals for treatment and released. Emergency response personnel from Washington, D.C., provided the on-scene treatment and transportation of the injured passengers.

As a result of its investigation of this accident, the Safety Board identified the following safety issues:

- Wheel-truing procedures
- Mitigating measures for wheel climb derailments
- WMATA interdepartmental coordination

As a result of its investigation of this accident, the National Transportation Safety Board makes recommendations to the Washington Metropolitan Area Transit Authority.

The National Transportation Safety Board determines that the probable cause of the January 7, 2007, derailment of Washington Metropolitan Area Transit Authority train 504 as it traversed a standard turnout track near the Mt. Vernon Square station in Washington, D.C., was a wheel climb on car 5152 that was initiated by a rough wheel surface created when the wheel was trued with a milling machine, the lack of quality control measures to ensure that wheel surfaces were smoothed after truing, the lack of a guard rail on the No. 8 turnout, and Washington Metropolitan Area Transit Authority's failure to have an effective process to implement safety improvements identified following similar accidents and related research projects.

FACTUAL INFORMATION

Accident Synopsis

On January 7, 2007, about 3:45 p.m. eastern standard time,[1] northbound Washington Metropolitan Area Transit Authority (WMATA) Metrorail train 504 derailed one car as the train traversed a crossover from track 2 to track 1. The accident occurred in an underground tunnel on the Metrorail Green Line near the Mt. Vernon Square 7th Street-Convention Center (Mt. Vernon Square) station at chain marker E2 23+28. The train was traveling about 18 mph as it approached the station.

The train consisted of six cars. The fifth car (5152) from the head end of the train derailed. About 80 passengers were on board at the time of the accident. Twenty-three passengers were transported to local hospitals for treatment and released. Emergency response personnel from Washington, D.C., provided the on-scene treatment and transportation of the injured passengers.

Accident Narrative

On the day of the accident, train 504, with six cars, departed northbound from the Branch Avenue Metrorail station on the Green Line. (See figure 1.) Car 5024 was in the lead followed by cars 5025, 5185, 5184, 5152, and 5153. The train was about 450 feet long, and the cars were equipped with event recorders.

The wheels on the lead truck of car 5152 had been trued,[2] or reprofiled, at the WMATA Greenbelt facility beginning on Friday night, January 5, 2007. The trailing truck wheels of car 5152 and all the wheels of car 5153 had been trued January 6, 2007. The cars then left the Greenbelt facility to become part of the accident train, which was returned to revenue service on Sunday, January 7, 2007, the day of the derailment.

---

[1] All times in this report are eastern standard time.

[2] Wheel *truing*, or reprofiling, recontours wheels that get flat spots, become out-of-round, or reach condemnable limits.

Figure 1. WMATA Metrorail system map.

Train 504 departed the Branch Avenue station at 3:15 p.m. instead of 3:06 p.m. as scheduled because trains were using only one track, or single tracking,[3] at the Mt. Vernon Square station. When it reached the L'Enfant Plaza station, train 504 was held to let two southbound trains pass through the single-tracking[4]

---

[3] In *single tracking*, trains traveling in opposite directions alternately share one track.

[4] The single-track operation between L'Enfant Plaza and Mt. Vernon Square was scheduled to take place on the day of the accident between 2:05 p.m. and midnight. The operation was cancelled after the derailment.

area. Train 504 was then taken out of automatic control and put in manual mode with speed commands. After closing the passenger doors for departure at L'Enfant Plaza, the train operator was unable to close the operator's window in the control cab. The train continued to the next station. At the Gallery Place/Chinatown station, the train operator saw a car maintenance worker on the platform and made an announcement requesting the worker to board the train. The car maintenance worker boarded the train and then used the intercom to communicate with the train operator. Next, as the train departed the station, the worker walked to the lead of the train to help with the inoperable window.

According to data from the event recorder, the train accelerated to 45 mph. As the train approached the crossover from track 2 to track 1 at Mt. Vernon Square, the operator slowed the train. When the lead car reached the station platform, the train stopped. (See figure 2.) The train operator heard someone on the platform[5] yelling that there was a derailment.

Figure 2. Front (left) and side (right) views of car 5152 where it struck tunnel wall.

---

[5] It became clear during the investigation that the person who yelled was the operator of the southbound train, which was stopped at the Mt. Vernon Square station platform.

At 3:45 p.m., the operator of a southbound train that was stopped at Mt. Vernon Square told Operations Central Control (OCC), which coordinates and dispatches all train movements on the Metrorail system, that there was a derailment at the Mt. Vernon Square station. Between 3:46 p.m. and 3:51 p.m., the OCC instructed the operator of train 504 and the car maintenance worker who was on the train to set the handbrakes on the train and verify which cars were derailed. The car maintenance worker reported to the OCC that the trailing car pair (the fifth and sixth cars) was derailed and that people remained on those cars. The OCC directed the car maintenance worker to enter the trailing pair and check the passengers for injuries. The first car in the train reached the platform, and passengers in the first four cars were able to exit the train through the first car and onto the platform. Because of damage to the fifth car, passengers in the fifth and sixth cars could not walk through the train and instead had to disembark at track level.

At 3:53 p.m., an OCC assistant superintendent called 911 and told the call taker about a report of a derailment at the Mt. Vernon Square station. The assistant superintendent said that there were no injuries reported at that time and requested fire department assistance for the rail cars derailed in the tunnel. The assistant superintendent also stated that passengers might need to be evacuated to the track.

At 3:55 p.m., a Metrorail employee at the Mt. Vernon Square station called 911 and said that an ambulance was needed for a passenger reporting back and neck pain who was at the kiosk on the mezzanine level.

The Washington, D.C., Fire and Emergency Medical Services Department began dispatching resources to the Mt. Vernon Square station at 3:57 p.m. The resources dispatched included a fire deputy, two battalion chiefs, five engine companies, two truck companies, two medic units, one emergency medical services unit, and three ambulances. Units began arriving at the station at 4:00 p.m.

At 4:23 p.m., an on-scene WMATA employee confirmed that the third rail power was down. The train evacuation of the two rear cars began at 4:26 p.m. and was completed at 4:47 p.m.

Injuries and Damages

Emergency response personnel from Washington, D.C., assessed the injured at the Mt. Vernon Square station. Twenty-three passengers reported being injured and were transported to area hospitals. None of the injuries was life threatening.

Track turnout damage was limited to a few permanent spring clips that needed to be replaced. No other significant switch components required replacement. The contact damage at the tunnel wall and track damage accounted for about $1,000 in damages. WMATA estimated that it would cost $3.8 million to replace the damaged vehicles.

Accident Location and Site Description

Track

The derailment occurred on the Green Line of the Metrorail System south of the Mt. Vernon Square station. This portion of the Green Line is in Washington, D.C.

Tracks are owned, inspected, maintained, and operated by WMATA. The Green Line, in the vicinity of the derailment, consists of two main tracks signaled for operations in either direction. Within the tunnel structure, a concrete wall separates the two tracks. The concrete wall has passageways or egress to both tracks.

The derailment occurred as northbound train 504 entered the standard right-hand No. 8 turnout[6] on main track 2 traveling about 18 mph. (A standard turnout differs from a guarded turnout because it lacks guard rails positioned along the switch's running switch point and running rail on the turnout side. WMATA maintains both guarded and unguarded, or standard, turnouts. See figure 3.) The train derailed three of the four axles of its fifth car at chain marker E2 23+24, which is located along the curved closure

Figure 3. Unguarded No. 8 turnout (top) and guarded No. 8 turnout (bottom).

---

[6] A *turnout* diverts trains from one track to another. The turnout number indicates the sharpness of the curve of the diverging track. The higher the turnout number, the shallower the curve.

rail of the turnout. This No. 8 turnout is part of an interlocking[7] that consists of two extended crossovers (double crossovers) joined in the middle of the two tracks at a rail crossing (diamond). This configuration allows routing of trains from each main track in either direction to cross over to the opposite main track. (See figure 4.)

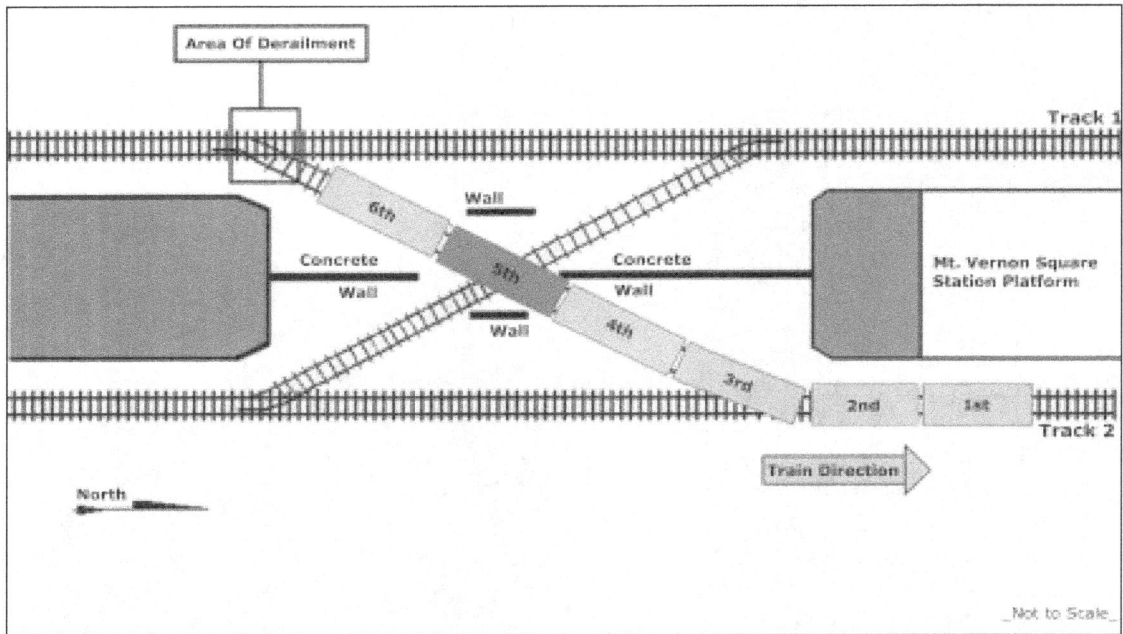

Figure 4. Track layout showing interlocking and station platform at the Mt. Vernon Square Metrorail station.

The maximum allowable operating speed for the track approaching the interlocking is 50 mph. Trains operating through the crossover where the derailment occurred are restricted to 22 mph, which is designated in the operating instructions and enforced by the signal system.

In the area of the derailment, the track is oriented in a north-south direction. The chain marker numbering increases in the northward direction. Between chain markers E2 18+57 and E2 22+96 the track is tangent. Between chain markers E2 18+57 and E2 21+00 the track is at a positive vertical grade of 3.99 percent, changes to 0.35 percent, and remains constant through the switch and station area.

The track structure in the area of the derailment is direct fixation, anchored in concrete. This type of construction is without ballast or conventional wooden crossties. There were no signs of improper drainage. The turnout where the derailment occurred contains the original material installed when the track was placed into service on May 11, 1991.

---

[7] *Interlocking* refers to an arrangement of signals, switch lock, and signal appliances interconnected so that their movements succeed each other in a predetermined order.

The rail through the accident site is 115-pound RE section Bethlehem Steel manufactured in 1986. The distance from the end of the switch point[8] to the point of frog[9] is 68 feet. (See figure 5.) The No. 8 turnout switch points measured 16 feet 6 inches. The stock rails and matching switch points are milled with a full undercut design and are supported with a set of switch plates (uniform risers) designed to allow for movement of the switch points.

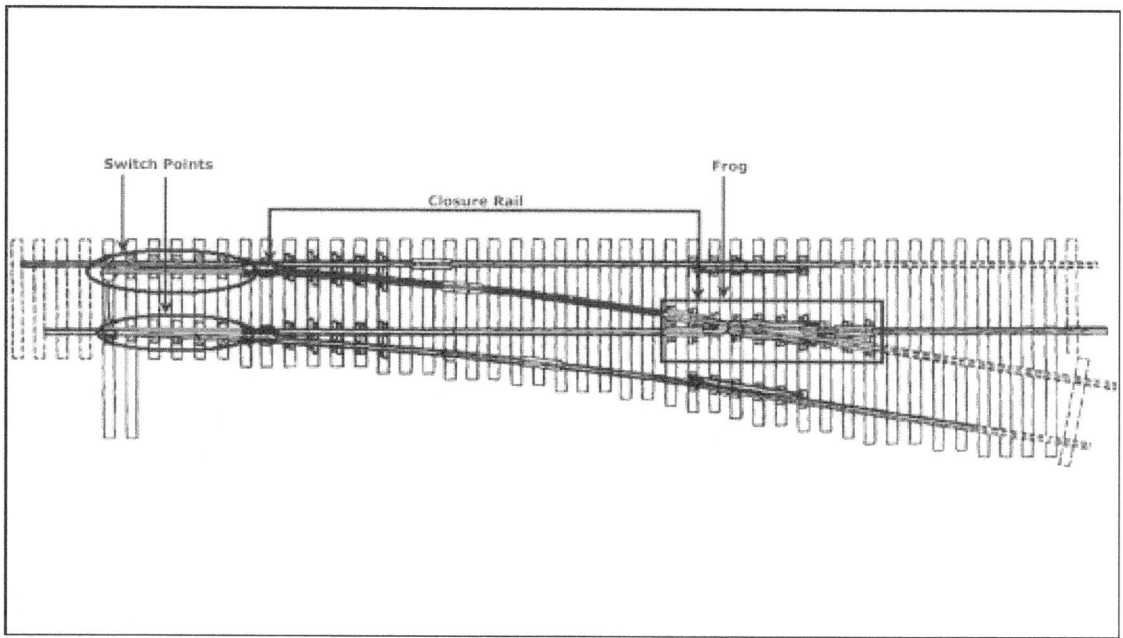

Figure 5. Typical track turnout showing component nomenclature.

Tunnel Structure

The track section of the Green Line between the Gallery Place/Chinatown station and the Mt. Vernon Square station is located in an underground tunnel that passes under H, I, L, and M Streets and Massachusetts and New York Avenues. The tunnel parallels or closely follows under 7th Street, NW. The tunnel construction south of the turnout area is circular, with a precast tunnel lining equipped with safety walkways. The circular design ends south of the turnout, where the tunnel design becomes a "box" tunnel construction. The derailed car contacted the leading corner of the center divider wall in the crossover.

---

[8] The *switch point* is the point where the gage line of the switch rail essentially intersects the gage line of the stock, or main, rail.

[9] A *frog* is used where two running rails intersect and provides flangeways to permit wheels and wheel flanges on either rail to cross the other rail. The *point of frog,* also called the 1/2-inch point of frog, is the point at which the spread between gage lines is 1/2 inch; all measurements are made from the point of frog.

Method of Operation and Signal Information

Train operations are governed by the *Metrorail Safety Rules and Procedures Handbook*, dated January 2004. All train control and supervision for the entire transit system is conducted through the OCC, which is located in Washington, D.C. The OCC is equipped with monitoring, control, and communication facilities required to operate the transit system and handle emergency situations.

Train operations on the Green Line are also governed by a traffic control system that controls train movements in both directions on the two main tracks. The system employs color-light signals at interlocking locations. Audio frequency track circuits control train speeds. Interlocking locations are operated remotely from a control panel in the OCC.

Train operations can be carried out by either automatic train control or manual control by a train operator. On the day of the accident, trains were running in automatic mode until they entered the single-track area, where they operated in manual mode with speed commands.

Metrorail runs an estimated 260 trains on weekdays, 165 trains on Saturdays, and 131 trains on Sundays. On the day of the derailment, 12 trains, including the accident train, used the accident crossover.

Train Equipment

General

Train 504 was made up of 5000-series cars designed and fabricated by Construcciones Y Auxiliar de Ferrocarriles (CAF) of Madrid, Spain. The 5000-series cars were delivered to WMATA between April 17, 2001, and June 11, 2004. The 192 cars in the series were numbered 5000 through 5191.

The cars were designed for operation in semi-permanent or "married" pairs of cars that were mechanically designated "A" or "B." Individual cars of a married pair cannot operate separately because the pair shares certain electronic control and other components necessary for operation. Each A- or B-car carries unique equipment that when "married" enables the pair to function as one unit. When a train was in service, only one operator compartment was occupied. Three married pairs were coupled together to form the accident train.

Each 5000-series car is about 75 feet long, 10 feet wide, and 10 feet 10 inches tall from the top of the rail and weighs about 77,500 pounds. The 5000-series cars were designed with 66 seats and to have a nominal "full load" capacity of 175 passengers.[10] The cars are constructed principally of aluminum alloy.

Braking, Running Gear, and Suspension

Braking. WMATA trains in revenue service generally run in automatic mode, which dictates braking rates of 2.2 mph/second (sec) in normal full service braking, 3.0 mph/sec in the "B-5" brake handle position, and 3.2 mph/sec in emergency braking. These braking rates are set at the limits of wheel-to-rail adhesion for dry conditions. Metrorail cars are equipped with a slip/slide detection system (also called a decelostat) designed to minimize wheel slip. However, depending on passenger load and rail surface condition—precipitation, dew, ice, blowing leaves, grease, contamination—wheels may slip or slide, and flat spots occur. Consequently, Metrorail car wheels generally are trued, or reprofiled, for flat spots rather than for wear.

Wheels. The cars involved in the accident were equipped with multiple-wear curved plate steel wheels that were a nominal 28 inches in diameter when new but that could be worn down to 25 inches in diameter before they needed replacement.[11]

Prior to 1978, WMATA Metrorail car wheels had cylindrical wheel profiles that resulted in excessive wheel and rail wear. Field experiments were conducted between 1978 and 1979 to find a wheel profile that caused less wear and performed better. Three 1000-series (Rohr) car wheels were machined with various profiles to determine which was optimal for wear and performance. The tests led to the adoption as the Metrorail standard of the "British Worn" wheel profile, which has a 63-degree wheel flange angle.

At the time of the accident, WMATA employed four wheel-reprofiling machines to recontour wheels that get flat spots or become out-of-round. Three of the machines were lathe machines that use one cutting tool that moves over a rotating wheel like a lathe to cut a new surface profile. The other machine was a milling machine with 144 bits mounted on a head that is shaped to cut a new wheel profile as the bits rotate into a slowly turning wheel surface. The milling machine left a relatively rougher "fish scale" pattern on the wheel tread and flange surfaces than the lathe-type machines, which left a smooth "record like" grooved surface. After wheels were cut, the machine operator coated the wheel flange with a lubricant, which was intended to prevent the newly cut surface from grabbing onto a rail curve and climbing to derailment. WMATA acknowledged

---

[10] The following defined loads for persons of 150 pounds each: Normal load (81 persons) - 12,150 pounds, Full load (175 persons) - 26,250 pounds, Crush load (232 persons) - 34,800 pounds, and Absolute maximum load (252 persons) - 37,800 pounds. Since the 5000-series cars were delivered, the American Public Transportation Association in March 2004 revised the standard weight used in these load calculations from 150 to 172 pounds.

[11] As wheel diameter changes, shims of varying thickness are used between the truck bolster and the car body to maintain a relatively constant car body height above the running rail.

that the milling machine surface, which was rougher than a lathe machine surface, might be more susceptible to wheel climb, a phenomenon known to the rail transit industry.

Trucks. The rail passenger car trucks are designed as a separate system from the car body. Two trucks (front and rear) supporting one car body make up one car. Each truck acts independently. While the truck supports the car body, passenger car trucks are designed to minimize the transfer of track-generated forces to the car body. This is primarily accomplished through three truck subsystems unique to passenger car trucks: the truck frame, an equalizing mechanism, and the suspension or cushioning system.

The truck frame is the transition piece between the car body and the moving parts of the truck. The frame also acts as a safety device; any one-wheel failure may be partially supported through the frame to the other three wheels until the train can be brought to a stop. There are two basic truck designs used on WMATA Metrorail cars. The trucks on the 1000-, 5000-, and 6000-series cars are a "Rockwell"[12] design. The trucks on the 2000-, 3000-, and 4000-series cars are a "Breda"[13] design. The Rockwell truck frame is constructed of two symmetrically opposing halves joined together by two transom bearings, which provide rigidity but still afford limited vertical movement. Thus the frame design incorporates a semi-rigid foundation that also includes an equalizing mechanism that helps ensure that all four wheels maintain contact with the rail during limited twisting or flexing during operation.

Any torsional movement between cars is minimized through the couplers and their related cushioning systems directly from car body to car body. Car couplers, both mechanical and semipermanently fixed between married pairs, are of a flexible design to allow independent movement between cars during normal service. The car body design of the 5000-series Metrorail cars was designed to be more robust and rigid than earlier Metrorail car models in order to provide greater crashworthiness in the event of a collision or accident. Therefore torsional movement or "twist" of a 5000-series car was considered to be less than that of previous models.

Air Spring Suspension/Leveling System. A pair of airbags (also called air springs) is located above each truck and provides secondary suspension at each corner of a car. Thus a 5000-series car has four-point air spring suspension. Compressed air is supplied to the suspension/leveling system from the main reservoir pipe. The air spring system was designed to provide optimal suspension and ride regardless of passenger load and to keep the car level regardless of load distribution under normal track conditions.

---

[12]   Named after the company that designed the truck, Rockwell International.

[13]   Breda Construzioni Ferroviarie S.p.A of Italy.

Control equipment for the air spring suspension/leveling system consists of a Knorr leveling valve for each air spring connected to a duplex check valve on each truck. The duplex check valve equalizes pressures between air spring pairs within 36 pounds per square inch (psi) (2.5 bar[14]) to prevent the vehicle from excessive leaning in the event of an air spring failure (deflation).

The air spring suspension system on the WMATA 5000-series cars has been problematic from delivery and has undergone a number of modifications. For example, WMATA found that the air spring linkage was inadequate and replaced it with a more flexible and longer wearing design. More important, WMATA found that the Knorr leveling valve had virtually no "dead band,"[15] or pressure tolerance, before air was added to or removed from its airbag. This caused each of the four valves on a car to adjust pressure constantly in response to the adjustments made by the other valves as the car's weight shifted with increases or decreases at the corners. Thus the valves were continuously working, and they wore out much sooner than planned. Also, the Knorr design made leveling of 5000-series cars extremely difficult during periodic inspections, even in the controlled environment of the maintenance facilities. As a result, WMATA modified its leveling procedure extensively and was exploring replacement of the Knorr valves with those manufactured by Westcode. At the time of the accident, the derailed car, 5152, had been fitted with overhauled Knorr leveling valves and the new linkage design and was thus considered by the WMATA staff to be in serviceable condition.

Personnel Information

Train Operator

The northbound train operator was hired by WMATA in September 2000 as a bus driver and worked in this capacity for about 1 1/2 years. She then transferred to rail service and worked as a station manager for about 8 months before becoming a train operator. She had been working in this position for about 5 years when the accident occurred. WMATA training records indicate that the train operator was up to date in rules training required for operating trains.

The train operator reported for duty at 7:04 a.m. at the Greenbelt rail yard on January 7, 2007. The train was out of the yard at 7:24 a.m. and departed the Greenbelt station at 7:34 a.m. The train operator made two round trips from the Greenbelt station to the Branch Avenue station on the Green Line. She then took a break at 11:24 a.m. at Greenbelt and was back on duty at 12:08 p.m. She was then assigned to train 504 and made the trip from Greenbelt to Branch Avenue. She did

---

[14] A *bar* is a unit of pressure equal to 105 newtons per square meter, or 0.98697 standard atmosphere.

[15] The *dead band* is the bandwidth designed into a valve where no command is accepted to either increase or decrease pressure. The Knorr valve's dead band is ± 1/2°, which is very small and, for practical purposes, nonexistent.

not recall anything remarkable about the previous trips and noted that all train systems were functioning properly.[16]

Senior Track Inspector

The senior track inspector, or track walker, was hired by WMATA in 1995 as a laborer and held progressively higher-level positions within the track structures system maintenance department. In 1997, he advanced to the position of Level AA track walker, which was the position he held on the day of the accident. WMATA training records indicate that the senior track inspector had completed right-of-way training and was up to date in rules training required to perform his job.

The senior track inspector inspects each track twice each week from the Congress Heights station to the Shaw-Howard U station, which includes the derailment area. This territory consists of both main tracks for about 6.3 miles. The senior track inspector recently had bid for this territory, and it had been assigned to him as lead inspector for about 2 weeks when the accident occurred.

The senior track inspector conducts walking inspections with another track walker. They walk track 1 on Sundays and Tuesdays and track 2 on Mondays and Thursdays. On Wednesdays they perform repairs. Both track walkers inspect the track and look out for trains as they walk against the direction of traffic. The senior track inspector said that they also look for defects and lubrication of all switches as they walk the track.

Wheel Milling Machine Operator

The wheel milling machine operator who milled the lead wheels of car 5152 was experienced with the wheel milling machine and had operated it for a number of years. An operating manual and other guides for the milling machine were available at the machine. The operator milled the lead truck wheels on car 5152 beginning on Friday night, January 5, 2007. The next day, January 6, the trailing truck wheels of car 5152 and all the wheels of car 5153 were trued. Then both cars left the Greenbelt facility to become part of the accident train, which returned to revenue service on Sunday, January 7, the day of the derailment.

The machine operator was hired by WMATA in November 1975 as a mechanic helper and held progressively higher-level positions within the car maintenance department. He advanced to mechanic level AA and was working in this position on the day of the accident. WMATA personnel records indicate that he had had more than 30 years of general wheel milling experience at WMATA, with more than 10 of those years working on a milling machine at the Greenbelt maintenance facility. Training records indicate the operator was current on training required for his position.

---

[16] The train operator was tested for drugs and alcohol. The test results were negative.

Track Information

Postaccident Track Inspections and Tests

The footprint of the derailment was studied, and there was a distinctive mark along the left-hand switch point 5 feet 10 inches from the end of the switch point that is characteristic of a wheel rising from the normal wheel-rail interface, also called a wheel climb. This mark was the point-of-rise and was located at chain marker E2 23+02. There was a continuous wheel marking on the top of the switch point going northward into the curve closure rail.[17] The point of derailment was located at chain marker E2 23+24 at a point on the curved closure rail that is 28 feet 7 inches north of the end of the switch point of the No. 8 turnout.

There were wheel markings into the gage of the track, outside of the curve closure rail, where a mark on the north edge of an insulated joint bar was observed, as well as markings continuing northward in the gage of the track from the point on the opposite rail. A pair of wheel markings on the switch continued in a north direction after the initial markings. Wheel markings continued through the frog area to the point of rest where the fifth car stopped.

Track geometry measurements of gage and crosslevel were recorded at 40 stations, including the accident location. The stations were measured 10 feet apart. All track geometry measurements were compliant with WMATA track standards.

On the day of the accident, track 1 and the accident switch at the derailment site were inspected by a WMATA track inspector about 12:45 p.m., about 3 hours before the accident. No defects were noted for the switch or adjacent area in the vicinity of the derailment. In addition, rail lubrication for the crossover tracks was inspected and deemed appropriate. After the accident, Safety Board investigators found lubrication on both the rail through the turnout where the accident occurred and on the lead wheel of the car that derailed. The WMATA engineering department's policy for mainline track inspection is to inspect them twice weekly with at least 1 day between inspections. All switches were inspected during normal track inspections.

Investigators reviewed track inspection records between chain marker E 052+16 and chain marker F 256+7 on the Green Line from October 2, 2006, to January 7, 2007. Individuals designated by WMATA conducted all track inspections. The previous 3 months of records were reviewed. Investigators found that WMATA maintenance records were properly maintained and readily available.

WMATA had installed standard No. 8 turnouts connecting main tracks 1 and 2 in 1991 at Mt. Vernon Square. WMATA has not changed any components of the crossovers since their installation.

---

[17] The *closure rail*, which is curved, is the rail between the switch point and a frog in a turnout.

Lubrication Procedures

In a memorandum dated October 25, 2005, on the subject of inspection practice that was to "be used as a guide to insure safe single tracking, crossover and turnout operations," WMATA provided some instructions regarding rail lubrication. This document requires that track inspectors who are inspecting turnouts "maintain adequate approved rail lubricants on all special service tracks and No. 8 unguarded turnouts at all times." Proper application of rail lubrication on standard No. 8 turnouts reduces the coefficient of friction as a train maneuvers through a turnout.

WMATA also drafted a standard operating procedure titled "Rail and Switch Lubrication, Wayside and Manual Application" and a track maintenance procedure (No. 3) with the same title. These documents expand on the instructions from the October 25, 2005, memorandum and provide technical guidance regarding the location, application procedures, and frequency of rail lubrication. These two documents have not been formally adopted or implemented.

Mechanical Information

Postaccident Equipment Inspections and Tests

The postaccident mechanical investigation began at the derailment site where the cars remained after coming to rest. Due to the limited space inside the tunnel and the dim tunnel lighting, the nonderailed lead car sets, cars 5024-5025 and 5185-5184, were moved to WMATA's Greenbelt maintenance facility. The derailed car and its pair, cars 5152-5153, were moved to WMATA's Branch Avenue facility for further inspection.

Investigators inspected the four nonderailed cars, noting wheel contour and condition along with the general condition of the cars and running gear. No unusual wear or any marks or defects were found.

Investigators inspected the derailed car and its pair. The linkage between the leveling valve and the truck of the derailed car was damaged as a result of the derailment. Investigators also measured the wheel diameters and profiles and measured the wheels for wear.

Wheels. The wheel surfaces of car 5152 displayed a "fish scale" appearance that is typical of wheels trued by milling operations. (See figure 6.) Pronounced ridges also were evident across the wheel tread, completely through the throat area, and up the entire inboard vertical surface of the flange.

Investigators noted that all wheels on the right side of derailed car 5152 and the front truck of car 5153 had about 1/16 inch of wear even though the wheels on both cars had been trued on January 5 and 6, just a few days before the accident.

Investigators also examined the milling machine used to mill the wheels on car 5152. The alignment of the cutting head on the right side was about 1/16 inch closer to the inside than required. Further examination of the milling machine found worn parts.

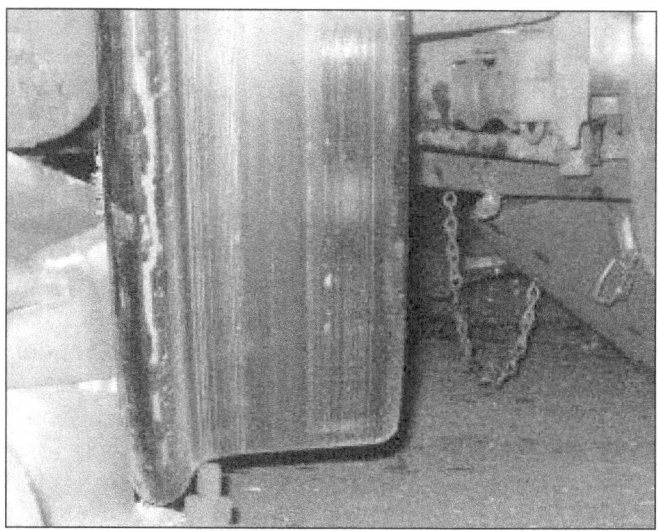

Figure 6. Wheel #2 from car 5152 with fish scale pattern from recent milling.

Safety Board investigators observed the wheels on a car being trued with the milling machine. Before beginning the milling operation, the machine operator did not index the cutting heads[18] to ensure that the wheel profile would be milled correctly. The machine operator said that WMATA did not have a standard schedule for indexing the heads; instead, indexing was done on an "as needed" basis. During the wheel-truing operation that investigators observed, the results proved unsatisfactory to the machine operator, and he then indexed the cutting heads and re-trued the wheels to obtain a satisfactory result.

From discussions with another transit agency that uses milling machines (Bay Area Rapid Transit District [BART]), investigators learned that it requires its milling machines to be indexed every day. Currently, WMATA milling machine operators determine satisfactory or unsatisfactory results subjectively. While there are specifications for wheel profile and wear limits, there are no explicit guidelines concerning the final surface texture.

Additionally, WMATA milling machine operators rebuild the cutting heads when required. The bits used by the milling machine are round with a hole through the center to attach them to the head. Both edges of the bits can be used so when a bit gets a nick or gouge on the cutting surface it can be reversed. Investigators examined the bits used for rebuilding the cutting heads. The bits were stored in three plastic coffee cans located on the workbench. One can was for new bits, one can for bits with one serviceable edge and one can for scrap bits. Investigators observed several bits in the wrong can.

---

[18] To *index the cutting heads* means to ensure that each bit has an undamaged surface locked in the cutting position. When any of the 144 bits on a cutting head (there are two on the WMATA milling machine) is damaged during cutting, it can be rotated to an undamaged cutting surface.

A rotational truck test was performed on the lead truck of the derailed car (5152) to determine whether there was abnormal resistance to rotation, which could cause or contribute to the wheel climb phenomenon. The force was within the range of many other nonderailed trucks previously measured and stored in WMATA's database.

Wheel/Rail Load Ratio. In 2005, WMATA installed a wheel/rail load detector (WRLD) near its Greenbelt maintenance facility to assess vehicle performance, identify poorly performing rail cars, and establish a database of wheel/rail forces. The detector determines truck performance as a car passes through the WRLD by measuring lateral loads, vertical loads, wheel angle of attack, lateral-to-vertical (L/V) load ratios, speed, and average car weight. Extensive computer vehicle performance simulations by Transportation Technology Center Incorporated (TTCI)[19] established parameters that are used to determine acceptable truck performance. The simulation results showed that L/V ratios should be less than 0.4 and that the L/V ratio of the lead axle of a car appeared to be the best discriminator for determining poorly performing cars. An L/V ratio higher than 0.4 indicates a car that steers poorly with hard flange contact and runs with the lead axle at a larger angle of attack.

Investigators reviewed WRLD L/V data recorded for cars 5152 and 5153 between December 7, 2006, and January 7, 2007. Of 36 recorded passages through the WRLD device, car 5152 had one L/V ratio recorded at 0.4 and eight recorded at more than 0.3, with the majority at or below 0.2. In the same time period, car 5153 had 12 L/V readings that were greater than 0.4, but none were higher than 0.4982. Most of the L/V readings were below 0.25. Just prior to the derailment, after wheel cutting and passing through the WRLD, neither car 5152 nor car 5153 had L/V readings higher than 0.25.

Derailment History and Research

Beginning April 17, 2003, several of WMATA's 5000-series cars experienced low-speed derailments in yards or on service tracks. The number of these was disproportionate compared to other series of Metrorail cars. By July 2006, seven derailments[20] that WMATA investigated had occurred in different locations, although two were in the same yard but on different tracks. All occurred at 15 mph or less, in temperatures between 40° and 100° Fahrenheit, with either lead and/or trailing wheels, and with wheel flange angles between 63 and 70.8 degrees. As a result of the derailments, WMATA assembled an internal committee, hired the TTCI as an outside consultant, and requested an American Public Transportation Association (APTA) technical review panel to convene.

---

[19] The *TTCI* is a subsidiary of the Association of American Railroads that conducts transportation research and testing.

[20] The dates and locations of the seven derailments are listed in appendix B.

The TTCI explored the significance of air spring pressure adjustment and stability to the performance of the 5000-series cars in two scenarios: one with a full pressure system but in an unbalanced condition, and one with a lower pressure (1 inch lower) in an unbalanced condition. The TTCI performed simulations for WMATA on the effect of vertical load unbalance for flange climb derailment of 5000-series cars with a new 70-degree wheel flange angle. The first simulations used an unbalanced condition of 10,000 pounds on diagonally opposite air spring vertical loads, which was consistent with a variation in air spring pressure from 31 psi to 71 psi. The unbalanced air spring condition increased the L/V ratio and risk of derailment compared to equally balanced air spring pressures. The simulations showed that the likelihood of derailment was even higher for wheels with a 63-degree wheel flange angle. They also predicted derailment on track curves with perturbations that have a friction coefficient of 0.6 and higher, and similar results were seen for the unbalanced condition in a standard No. 8 turnout.

In addition, the TTCI explored the effect of an unbalanced 1-inch height reduction below design for the 5000-series cars using wheels with a 70-degree wheel flange angle. This was done because the 1-inch-lower spring height was consistent with spring heights observed on a 5000-series car during characterization tests. By design, air spring compression of 1.29 inches creates contact with the emergency spring, which is much stiffer than the air spring. Thus any unbalanced condition that decreases or compresses the air springs an additional 0.29 inches over the 1-inch height reduction creates contact with the emergency spring. It was expected that such contact would significantly increase the potential for derailment. However, the simulation results showed almost no difference from the previous derailment potential with the unbalanced air springs at full system compression.

On July 30, 2004, a WMATA officer in the Office of Quality Assurance in the Department of System Safety and Risk Protection sent a memorandum to the new car purchase program manager for the 6000-series car purchases regarding 5000- and 6000-series car leveling valves. The memorandum presented a history of the failure of the Knorr leveling valves that were installed on the 5000-series Metrorail cars. The memorandum concluded that Knorr leveling valves should not be installed on future 6000-series cars and should be removed from 5000-series cars already in service.

On August 8, 2004, the new car purchase program manager for the 6000-series cars, who would later become the senior program manager responsible for all new car procurement and car renovation, replied to the memorandum that it was very premature to react to the data. The 6000-series program manager did not alter current designs, preferring to wait until the Knorr valve is conclusively proved to be unsatisfactory and further discussions with the car builder. Discussions are ongoing between WMATA's car maintenance and vehicle engineering departments over inclusion of the Knorr valve in the 7000-series car currently being designed.

As a temporary measure, WMATA created a new leveling procedure. In addition, WMATA replaced the linkage between the truck and the valve, which maintains car height, with a different design. Despite these efforts, the car leveling issue has not been resolved.

In August 2005, the Transportation Research Board's Transit Cooperative Research Program (TCRP)[21] published *Report 71, Track-Related Research, Volume 5: Flange Climb Derailment Criteria and Wheel/Rail Profile Management and Maintenance Guidelines for Transit Operations.*[22] This report discussed flange climb derailment factors for transit vehicles and practices to reduce the risk of wheel climb, such as quality control of wheel-truing procedures, lubrication of rails, and installation of guarded turnouts. A guarded turnout, or switch, has a restraining guard rail adjacent to the inside running rail. Contact between the inside face of the wheel rim and the restraining guard rail prevents the opposite wheel from pushing against the outside rail as the car maneuvers through a turnout, thus physically restraining the outside wheel from climbing the rail.

WMATA provided investigators with a switch inventory document indicating that at the time of the accident it maintained 75 guarded No. 8 turnouts and 98 standard (unguarded) No. 8 turnouts on the main tracks of the Metrorail system. WMATA noted that it is replacing all standard No. 8 turnouts on main track with guarded No. 8 turnouts during the normal replacement cycle. It installed about 15 guarded No. 8 turnouts in 2005 and 34 in 2006. The projected goal for 2007 is 30, and WMATA had already completed 26 as of September 2007.[23] WMATA described the order of turnout replacement as "going after the worst turnouts first," based on degree of wear.

The TCRP report researched wheel surface characteristics in relation to wheel climb derailments and stated that a rough wheel surface finish from wheel reprofiling increases the probability of a wheel climb derailment.[24] The report further indicated that wheel surface conditions may be improved by addressing the final wheel surface. Addressing the final wheel surface can involve a light finishing cut, with no significant material removed, to smooth the roughness of the wheel tread surface. Newly trued wheels can be smoothed by running the cars through yard tracks until the rough finish is removed.

In October 2005, the TTCI provided WMATA its *Wheel-Rail Interface Study,* P-05-056. The study was aimed primarily at determining the effect on the propensity for wheel flange climb derailment of the 1000-, 2000-, and 5000-series Metrorail

---

[21] The *TCRP* was established under Federal Transit Administration sponsorship in July 1992 and provides a forum where transit agencies can cooperatively address common operational problems.

[22] This report was one of seven on track-related research. The research for this report was conducted "to improve wheel/rail interaction in transit systems by introducing flange climb derailment criteria and wheel/rail profile management and maintenance guidelines that can be applied to transit operations."

[23] As of September 2007, WMATA had 101 guarded and 72 standard No. 8 turnouts on the main tracks of the Metrorail system.

[24] Transportation Cooperative Research Program, *Report 71, Track-Related Research, Volume 5: Flange Climb Derailment Criteria and Wheel/Rail Profile Management and Maintenance Guidelines for Transit Operations* (Washington, DC: TRB, 2005) A-3.

cars of a wheel profile with a 63-degree wheel flange angle as compared to a 70-degree wheel flange angle. Among the report's conclusions were the following:

- With the existing British Worn wheel with a 63-degree wheel flange angle, there is a significant risk of a flange climb derailment, even on vehicles in their as-designed condition, when operating on curves below 320-foot radius or No. 8 turnouts.

- Risk of derailment with British Worn wheel with a 63-degree wheel flange angle is increased in the presence of track irregularities that are within existing WMATA track geometry standards.

- With worn British Worn wheels, with a 70-degree gage face angle and rails that are worn to a 70-degree wheel flange angle, there is little risk of a flange climb derailment with vehicles in the as-designed condition even with track irregularities that were evaluated in the assessment.

- The new TTCI-designed 70-degree wheel flange angle profile significantly reduces the risk of a flange climb derailment compared to the existing British Worn profile on new or worn rail.

- Higher levels of wheel/rail friction generate increased L/V ratios, increasing the risk of flange climb derailment.

- Air spring vertical load unbalance similar to that measured in WMATA can greatly increase the risk of flange climb derailment. This is possible on the 2000- and 5000-series cars, which have four leveling valves, but is not possible on the 1000-series cars with three leveling valves.

- Having air spring heights up to 1 inch lower than the design did not seem to have a significant influence on the propensity for derailment under the conditions simulated. However, the increased probability of emergency spring contact that results from this condition could increase the risk of derailment scenarios that were not investigated in this limited study.

The TTCI made recommendations in the October 2005 report, including the following:

- WMATA should instigate as soon as possible its informally stated requirement that all yard curves with radii less than 500 feet should be equipped with restraining rails. This should also apply to No. 8 turnouts (and sharper). This improvement would significantly reduce the low speed derailments in yards and turnouts/switches.

- WMATA should implement a program to reduce vertical spring imbalance in the 2000- and 5000-series cars.

- Simulations of air spring imbalance and low air spring height were performed for a very limited set of conditions. Further simulations could be conducted to obtain a better understanding of the effects of air spring imbalance, different combinations of air spring height, and air-spring lap band for a variety of track geometric conditions.

- WMATA should adopt the new wheel profile recommended by the TTCI to reduce the risk of flange climb derailment under normal operating conditions.

On March 13, 2007, the APTA Technical Review Panel issued its final report to WMATA regarding factors relating to the cause of the derailments of the 5000-series cars and how to prevent future derailments. The report listed the following contributing factors:

1. Friction coefficient between the wheel and rail,

2. Wheel flange geometry,

3. Rail gage face geometry,

4. Vertical and lateral load at the interface of the wheel and rail, and

5. Angle of attack of the wheel against the rail as driven by lateral load.

The APTA report stated that wheel flange geometry and rail gage-face geometry were "not likely the unique cause of the 5000-series car derailments." The report identified "angle of attack of the wheel against the rail" as an area for further investigation and monitoring.

Of all the contributing factors, APTA identified "vertical and lateral load at the interface of the wheel and rail" as the most likely unique factor that contributed to the 5000-series car derailments. APTA said that the "problematic and unreliable" air suspension system setup was a key component in the distribution of weight in a car. APTA noted further that

> The fact that it was reported that 75 percent of the [car] weight was supported on diagonally opposite corners almost certainly was the reason the one car derailed. Since adjustment is virtually impossible to obtain, it is possible, and even likely, that adjustments will be made which will result in car weight distributions which are even more erroneous.

The APTA report made recommendations in the areas of wheel loading, yaw resistance of the truck, and wheel and rail profile. The wheel loading recommendation included the use of a leveling valve with a wider dead band, use of a three-valve rather than the current four-valve leveling system, and concurrent development of a new leveling procedure. The truck yaw resistance recommendation questioned the adequacy of the current side bearing modification program, the cause of rusted center pins, and the wear of the center pin liner. The wheel and rail profile recommendation suggested that WMATA consider changing the wheel profile, reviewing track requirements in the WMATA *Track Standards Manual*, and enhancing rail lubrication efforts. The report noted that lubrication improvements to reduce the coefficient of friction between wheel and rail would make derailments less likely to occur and noted further that WMATA had enhanced wheel-rail lubrication during the past several years.

APTA also made some general observations, including the following:

- The problematic Knorr leveling valves were having problems at the same time the newer 6000-series cars were being delivered by Alstom with the same valves.

- Car maintenance personnel input was either not solicited or listened to during the design and engineering process for new cars, nor was there a comprehensive process to include all departments in the specification review process for new cars and equipment.

- The WMATA car fleet defect level of about 15 percent is reflective of chronic equipment design and specification problems, such as the leveling valves, compared to New York City Transit, which has a 5-percent defect level.

- The current WMATA derailment investigation process, while very comprehensive, takes an inordinate amount of time to complete.

- There seems to be no single point of responsibility for determining what actions will be taken as a result of the derailment investigations nor a clear means by which corrective action will be monitored.

ANALYSIS

Exclusions

Safety Board investigators inspected the WMATA track and reviewed the signal system data logs. No anomalies that would have caused or contributed to the derailment were identified. Signal system data indicated that the signals were functioning properly at the time of the accident.

Each transit car was examined. Safety Board investigators performed rotational stiffness (yaw) tests on the lead truck of car 5152 to determine whether it contributed to or initiated a wheel climb. The tests indicated that the lead truck of car 5152 was performing within the parameters of the rest of the fleet.

The Safety Board concludes that the following were not factors in the accident: the operation of the train; the condition of the track; the track geometry; the signal system; the switch point and switch maintenance; and truck rotation stiffness.

Investigation

Safety Board investigators examined the standard No. 8 turnout (crossover track) where the derailment occurred and noted a distinctive mark where the wheel began to rise along the face and on top of the left-hand switch point rail 5 feet 10 inches from the end of the switch point. Wheel markings continued on top of the rail for 22 feet 9 inches before dropping to the outside of the rail. Event recorder data indicate that train speed was appropriate, and postaccident inspections revealed no anomalies or defects in the crossover track where the derailment occurred. The Safety Board concludes that distinctive wheel markings on the rail show that the lead wheel on the lead truck of the fifth car climbed over the outer rail in a standard No. 8 turnout. The investigation examined factors and conditions that may have contributed to the wheel climb derailment and actions that can reduce the likelihood of a wheel climb.

Wheels

The wheels on the fifth car had been trued at WMATA's Greenbelt maintenance facility 2 days prior to the derailment using a milling machine, and the car had been returned to train service the day of the accident. The surface of the wheel that climbed the rail displayed a "fish scale" appearance and had pronounced ridges. The only smooth, polished area was about a 1/4-inch-wide line in the center where the wheel tread most frequently made contact with the rail head. WMATA milling machine operators did not polish wheel surfaces after truing operations. The TCRP report[25] indicates that a rough wheel surface finish from wheel truing increases the probability of a wheel climb derailment. The report further indicates that wheel surface conditions may be improved by addressing the final wheel surface. Addressing the final wheel surface can involve a light finishing cut, with no significant material removed, to smooth the roughness of the wheel tread surface. Newly trued wheel surfaces can also be polished by running the cars through curved yard tracks and turnouts until the rough finish is smoothed over the entire tread surface. The Safety Board concludes that WMATA's lack of measures to smooth wheel surfaces after truing increases the potential for a wheel climb derailment. WMATA has no explicit guidelines concerning the final surface texture. The Safety Board therefore believes that WMATA should develop a standard for maximum allowable wheel roughness and develop and implement post-wheel-truing procedures to meet that standard.

Transit industry research indicates that wheel surface conditions are improved by frequently inspecting the cutting tools, especially on wheel-milling machines. However, WMATA did not have a standard schedule for inspecting and indexing the milling machine cutting heads; instead, indexing was done on an "as needed" basis. From discussions with another transit agency that uses milling machines (BART), investigators learned that it requires its milling machines to be indexed every day.

The investigation found irregularities in the dimensions of recently trued wheels at WMATA, including the wheel that derailed in this accident. Although the overall profile of the wheel was accurate, measurements indicated that more material was being removed during the truing operation than was necessary. The cutting head on the milling machine that was used on the wheel was found to be out of alignment. The milling machine's internal bearings were replaced, and the alignment was corrected. The Safety Board concludes that although the misalignment of the milling machine used in WMATA's wheel-truing operation did not contribute to the wheel climb, it does indicate inadequacies in WMATA's quality assurance process. The Safety Board therefore believes that WMATA should implement quality assurance procedures to ensure accurate wheel truing, including the regular alignment and indexing of cutting heads on wheel milling machines.

Another factor considered in evaluating the potential for a wheel climb derailment is the wheel flange angle. The October 2005 TTCI report provided to WMATA concluded that there is a significant risk of a wheel climb derailment in a standard No. 8 turnout with the existing British Worn wheel with a 63-degree wheel flange angle. It also noted that there is little risk of a flange climb derailment with wheels and rails that are worn to a 70-degree flange angle, even with track

---

[25] TCRP, *Flange Climb Derailment Criteria*, A-3.

irregularities that were examined. WMATA has not taken steps to change the wheel profiles on its system at this time. Changing the wheel profile to 70 degrees would change the wheel-rail interface, would require reprofiling all of WMATA's wheels, and would likely necessitate rail head grinding to match the new wheel profile.

Although the TTCI report indicated that the 70-degree wheel angle would reduce the propensity for wheel climb, WMATA's 1000- through 4000-series cars also use wheels with a 63-degree flange angle, and those cars have not experienced similar wheel climb issues. The investigation found that at least one other transit agency, BART, uses the 63-degree wheel, and it has not reported similar problems with wheel climb derailments.

Car Leveling System

Problems with the car-leveling system on the 5000-series cars were identified soon after WMATA began taking delivery of the cars in 2001. Initially, adjustments were made to the linkage between the leveling valve and the truck. When this proved unsuccessful, modifications were made to the linkage. The modifications did not resolve the situation, so replacement valves were considered. Investigators found that concerns with the car-leveling system appeared to be common knowledge, and while varied attempts have been made, the car imbalance problem has not yet been resolved.

The APTA Technical Review Panel that was convened at the request of WMATA reviewed the seven prior low-speed derailments that involved the 5000-series cars. The panel found that up to 98 percent of the fleet of 5000-series cars failed a car-leveling check that was made during routine preventative maintenance procedures. Further, wheel loading could be 25 percent on one corner of a car and 75 percent on the diagonally opposite corner, an imbalance that could lead to a low-speed wheel climb derailment.

The APTA panel expressed concern that the same Knorr leveling valve in the 5000-series cars was also specified in the new 6000-series of WMATA Metrorail cars. The panel further noted its concern that WMATA interdepartmental communication was inadequate, stating that car maintenance personnel input was either not solicited or listened to during the design and engineering process for new cars, and there was no comprehensive process to include all relevant departments in the specification review process for new cars and equipment.

BART has passenger cars similar to the 5000-series cars used by WMATA. However, BART uses the Westcode leveling valve, which has a broader dead band than the Knorr valve, and BART also polishes newly trued wheel surfaces by running the cars through curved yard tracks until the wheels are smoothed across the tread surface. It is difficult to assess the performance of specific leveling valves in different transit systems and operating environments. Additionally, the leveling valve and associated linkage were damaged in the accident and could not be tested after the accident. Consequently, the extent to which the leveling system and/or valves may be a factor that increased the possibility for a wheel climb derailment at Mt. Vernon Square could not be determined.

WMATA has informed the Safety Board that it has recently installed instrumentation to collect on-board data to further examine and identify the problems with the leveling system on 5000-series cars. Nevertheless, the Board is concerned that inadequate communication between car maintenance department personnel and vehicle engineering design personnel may have delayed bringing this issue to resolution. The Board is also concerned that WMATA has taken delivery of more than 100 new 6000-series cars with car leveling systems equipped with Knorr valves and is in the process of preparing design specifications for a new 7000-series car, with the unresolved issues still associated with these valves. The Safety Board therefore believes that WMATA should establish procedures to ensure that there is appropriate coordination between all departments responsible for car maintenance and engineering design to ensure that problematic issues are identified, examined, and resolved before new equipment is ordered.

WMATA was aware of the wheel climb derailment problem with the 5000-series cars before this accident. Transit industry research and discussions with WMATA management indicate WMATA was aware of work done by the Transportation Research Board for the National Academy of Science and National Academy of Engineering on flange climb derailments in transit operations. Additionally, WMATA commissioned, participated in, and received the final *Wheel-Rail Interface Study* from the TTCI. Extensive testing to determine the cause of these relatively similar derailments in the 5000-series cars failed to produce a solid answer. Also, the APTA panel concluded that there was no single cause in the seven derailments it examined; however, the panel did identify several specific factors and made recommendations for WMATA to consider to prevent future derailments. Nonetheless, after requesting reviews by industry experts and funding related research work, WMATA failed to effectively address the proposed safety recommendations before this accident. The Safety Board therefore believes that WMATA should establish a process, including a single point of responsibility, to prompt timely evaluation and action on proposed safety improvements that are identified as a result of accident and derailment investigations and related research projects.

Rail Lubrication

Although the turnout where the accident occurred was adequately lubricated, the study of the previous yard derailments identified the application of rail lubrication on unguarded No. 8 turnouts as an important strategy to minimize the possibility of a wheel climb derailment. Proper rail lubrication on standard No. 8 turnouts, whether in a yard or on main track, reduces the coefficient of friction as a train maneuvers through a turnout, thereby reducing the potential for a wheel climb.

On October 25, 2005, WMATA sent a memorandum to track inspectors that requires them to assess the lubrication at all switches during routine track inspections. Track inspectors typically apply lubrication at turnouts, as needed, in accordance with the training and instructions detailing where to apply the lubrication. The memorandum emphasizes proper lubrication at crossovers and turnouts to ensure safe single-tracking operations.

Single tracking can occur at any time for a variety of reasons during normal operations and on days when routine track inspections are not conducted. Operating department personnel responsible for planning single-track operations determine the particular turnouts that will be utilized. Track engineering department personnel are responsible for lubricating switches as required during each inspection to ensure that the turnout remains adequately lubricated during a single-tracking operation. However, engineering personnel are not automatically notified when single-tracking operations are initiated. Because more trains are operated through lubricated switches utilized in single tracking, lubrication is depleted faster, which could eventually lead to an undesirable "dry rail" condition that increases the coefficient of friction and thereby increases the potential for a wheel climb derailment.

WMATA's October 25, 2005, memorandum does not contain requirements for coordination between the operating and track engineering departments. In addition, although WMATA has drafted a written standard operating procedure and a written track maintenance procedure that expand on the instructions in the memorandum and provide technical guidance regarding the location, application procedures, and frequency of rail lubrication, these procedures also do not address the need for interdepartmental communication and coordination when single-tracking operations are planned.

Because more frequent lubrication will likely be needed on turnouts used for single-track operations due to increased train traffic, when track department personnel are aware that a single-track operation is scheduled between track inspections, they can make arrangements for additional inspections to assess the adequacy of lubrication during the operation. The Safety Board concludes that although rail lubrication was not a factor in this accident, because a lack of rail lubrication can significantly increase the potential for wheel climb derailments, comprehensive rail lubrication procedures and interdepartmental coordination are needed that take into account both operational and track engineering demands. The Safety Board believes that WMATA should establish written procedures for rail lubrication that include close coordination between the operating and track engineering departments to ensure timely and appropriate rail lubrication is applied in normal and single-track operations.

Guarded Turnouts

The seven prior WMATA derailments, beginning in 2003, involved empty trains traveling at low speeds on yard tracks. Three of the derailments involved trains traversing standard (unguarded) No. 8 turnouts; the other four derailments occurred when a train maneuvered through a curve with a radius of less than 500 feet. Some of these derailments also involved cars that had recently had at least one set of wheels trued at a WMATA maintenance facility.

Guarded turnouts have an additional guard rail system that physically restrains the wheel sets from climbing the rail when a change in the wheel/rail interface occurs as a train traverses a turnout. Therefore, if an increased coefficient of friction from a rough wheel surface or a car imbalance occurs in a guarded turnout, the possibility of a wheel climb derailment is eliminated. The Safety Board concludes that had a guarded turnout been installed, it would have prevented the wheel climb and derailment of the fifth car as the accident train traversed the curved track.

The TTCI, APTA, and TCRP reports found that there is an increased risk of a wheel flange climb derailment when a transit car operates through a standard No. 8 turnout. Further, the TTCI report recommended in 2005 that WMATA replace standard No. 8 turnouts with guarded turnouts. WMATA has informed the Safety Board that it is replacing all standard No. 8 turnouts with guarded turnouts on its main track. Currently, WMATA is replacing an average of about 30 turnouts per year.

As of September 2007, WMATA had 101 guarded No. 8 turnouts and 72 standard (unguarded) No. 8 turnouts on the main tracks of the Metrorail system. Although the Safety Board recognizes that WMATA is making progress in replacing standard turnouts with guarded turnouts, the Board believes that WMATA should expedite and complete by 2009 the replacement of all No. 8 standard turnouts with guarded turnouts on main track.

CONCLUSIONS

Findings

1. The following were not factors in the accident: the operation of the train; the condition of the track; the track geometry; the signal system; the switch point and switch maintenance; and truck rotation stiffness.

2. Distinctive wheel markings on the rail show that the lead wheel on the lead truck of the fifth car climbed over the outer rail in a standard No. 8 turnout.

3. The Washington Metropolitan Area Transit Authority's lack of measures to smooth wheel surfaces after truing increases the potential for a wheel climb derailment.

4. Although the misalignment of the milling machine used in the Washington Metropolitan Area Transit Authority's wheel-truing operation did not contribute to the wheel climb, it does indicate inadequacies in the Washington Metropolitan Area Transit Authority's quality assurance process.

5. Although rail lubrication was not a factor in this accident, because a lack of rail lubrication can significantly increase the potential for wheel climb derailments, comprehensive rail lubrication procedures and interdepartmental coordination are needed that take into account both operational and track engineering demands.

6. Had a guarded turnout been installed, it would have prevented the wheel climb and derailment of the fifth car as the accident train traversed the curved track.

Probable Cause

The National Transportation Safety Board determines that the probable cause of the January 7, 2007, derailment of Washington Metropolitan Area Transit Authority train 504 as it traversed a standard turnout track near the Mt. Vernon Square station in Washington, D.C., was a wheel climb on car 5152 that was initiated by a rough wheel surface created when the wheel was trued with a milling machine, the lack of quality control measures to ensure that wheel surfaces were smoothed after truing, the lack of a guard rail on the No. 8 turnout, and Washington Metropolitan Area Transit Authority's failure to have an effective process to implement safety improvements identified following similar accidents and related research projects.

RECOMMENDATIONS

As a result of its investigation of the January 7, 2007, derailment of Washington Metropolitan Area Transit Authority Metrorail train 504 near the Mt. Vernon Square station in Washington, D.C., the National Transportation Safety Board makes the following safety recommendations:

To the Washington Metropolitan Area Transit Authority:

Develop a standard for maximum allowable wheel roughness and develop and implement post-wheel-truing procedures to meet that standard. (R-07-23)

Implement quality assurance procedures to ensure accurate wheel truing, including the regular alignment and indexing of cutting heads on wheel milling machines. (R-07-24)

Establish procedures to ensure that there is appropriate coordination between all departments responsible for car maintenance and engineering design to ensure that problematic issues are identified, examined, and resolved before new equipment is ordered. (R-07-25)

Establish a process, including a single point of responsibility, to prompt timely evaluation and action on proposed safety improvements that are identified as a result of accident and derailment investigations and related research projects. (R-07-26)

Establish written procedures for rail lubrication that include close coordination between the operating and track engineering departments to ensure timely and appropriate rail lubrication is applied in normal and single-track operations. (R-07-27)

Expedite and complete by 2009 the replacement of all No. 8 standard turnouts with guarded turnouts on main track. (R-07-28)

BY THE NATIONAL TRANSPORTATION SAFETY BOARD

Mark V. Rosenker
Chairman

Deborah A. P. Hersman
Member

Robert L. Sumwalt
Vice Chairman

Kathryn O'Leary Higgins
Member

Steven R. Chealander
Member

Adopted: October 16, 2007

Kathryn O'Leary Higgins, Member, filed the following concurring statement on October 23, 2007.

I concur with the findings, probable cause, and the recommendations made in this report on the derailment of one car of Washington Metropolitan Area Transit Authority train 504 near Mount Vernon Square Station in Washington, D.C., on January 7, 2007. While I agree with our report and recommendations, I continue to be concerned about two issues: the time that passed before passengers on the last two cars were evacuated; and the need for WMATA to identify a single point of responsibility to ensure that all of our safety recommendations are implemented.

We were fortunate that only 23 of the passengers on board the train that afternoon were transported to the hospital with non-life threatening injuries. I appreciate the staff's review and assurances that WMATA has emergency evacuation procedures in place and that those procedures were followed on the afternoon and evening of the accident. Yet, it was more than an hour from the time of the derailment until the evacuation of the two rear cars was completed, and more than 20 minutes from the time the evacuation started until it was completed. These incidents test our responses in real time, and provide valuable insight for future events. I believe we could have done more to learn what was done and why it was done. We learn important lessons from our investigations and I think we missed a chance to learn much more about emergency response from this incident.

We make important recommendations in this report, asking for procedures to ensure coordination and resolution of safety issues and a process to evaluate and act on safety improvements. I agree wholeheartedly with these recommendations because our investigation clearly showed that important safety improvements that could have prevented this accident were not made. Our recommendations make it clear new procedures and processes must be established to ensure that similar problems are avoided in the future. But new procedures and processes will not be effective unless a single point of responsibility is identified to assure that procedures are implemented and followed and conflicts are resolved. I urge WMATA to consider seriously the discussion in the Board Meeting that led to these important recommendations and adopt them as soon as possible.

Member Hersman joined Member Higgins in this statement.

APPENDIX A

Investigation

The National Transportation Safety Board was notified of the derailment of WMATA Metrorail train 504 in Washington, D.C., about 3:50 p.m. on January 7, 2007. The investigator-in-charge and the mechanical group chairman were launched from the Safety Board's Washington, D.C., headquarters office. The track group chairman was launched from the Chicago regional office. Kathryn O'Leary Higgins was the Board Member on scene. Investigative groups were formed to study mechanical equipment, track, and event recorder issues.

Parties to the investigation included WMATA and the Tri-State Oversight Committee.

APPENDIX B

Previous 5000-series Car Derailments

Date	Location	Car
April 17, 2003	Alexandria Yard - service track	5057
December 9, 2003	Alexandria Yard - service track	5062
August 19, 2004	Silver Spring Station - pocket track	5186
October 8, 2004	West Falls Church Yard	5138
April 10, 2006	New Carrolton Station - yard entrance track	5183
June 1, 2006	Branch Avenue Yard	5099
July 30, 2006	Brentwood Yard	5007